Job Search Essentials 3.0

Finding Your Next Career Adventure

Jim Wilson

Brooke DePue

Published by PathForeWord

http://www.PathForeWord.com

Copyright 2016

by James B. Wilson, Jr. and Brooke M. DePue

Foreword

In 2013, Jim began developing a considerable bit of expertise on the job search process based on being outsourced. He worked with some of the best outplacement consultants, job search workshops, and job search networks. He started the blog PathForeWord and pulled together all the critical information on the job search process for his readers.

He published Job Search Essentials that year and in late 2014 updated it with a new edition, Job Search Essentials 2.0.

In 2015, Brooke began work as a university career information specialist, working with students daily on their resumes, conducting monthly resume workshops, coaching students and alumni, as well as working with employers in job fairs and other events.

Given that background, we've combined our efforts and insight to develop this edition of Job Search Essentials, now version 3.0.

We hope you find this book valuable on your PathForeWord.

Jim Wilson, B.A.S., M.A., M.B.A.

Brooke DePue, B.S., M.S.

Table of Contents

Introduction

Job search can be an exciting time or it can be extremely frustrating. No doubt it's both of these during the course of a search that can be expected to take several months or longer.

If you're recently unemployed, we can empathize with your position. We've both been there, done that, and expect to encounter it again in our careers. It's a sad fact of life in the dynamic world of work that includes inevitable disruptions due to the economy or advancing technology. And, yes, it could also include personality disruptions.

If you're about to conclude your college education, you're very much focused on finding that first job, which includes weaving your college work and part-time employment into a cohesive package to present to prospective employers.

Ideally, you're thinking about your job search as a never-ending process throughout your career, whether you're employed or not. It needs to be a continuous effort of developing your network and honing your resume and LinkedIn profile. It's also wise to continue to develop your interviewing skills. That can easily include your tasks as both interviewee and interviewer, as the tables turn and you're trying to hire someone.

This book is about the essentials of that job search. It is a perfect guide to developing all the elements of your search and making just the right impression with your resume and LinkedIn profile, your cover letter, and during the interview.

Networking

The most important part of your job search will be networking. People hire people they know or who others that they know recommend. Get out and start connecting with all those you've worked with and whom you come into contact with through job search focus groups, industry associations, etc. Then never ever stop networking even after you've found your next stop on your PathForeWord.

You can read the stats and listen to the testimonials. From those it's clear that you find jobs and other opportunities through your connections. So the logic is to build your network of connections. In today's digital world, those connections can be readily facilitated through LinkedIn. Even so, how do you really find those connections? How do you make them work for your job search?

In order to make connections work you need to have a targeted plan for your job campaign. What job or position are you seeking? In what industry? What targeted companies? Once these key questions have been answered as part of your thoughts and planning, it becomes a great deal easier to determine who to contact and what help you need to make the desired connections.

Note, too, that this is clearly a two-way connection street that you're traveling. When working with your network, always include the statement "how can I help you?" This is particularly true as you build that network across job search focus groups or career transition workshops or better yet at industry association meetings.

LinkedIn

While many social networks are growing in importance for your job search, chiefly around networking, at the very top of any list has to be LinkedIn.

This is where your complete professional network lives, where your professional associations host conversations in their groups, and where the organizations with the jobs you want recruit new employees.

LinkedIn currently has more than 400 million members. Harnessing their connections can be just as much help to your job search as your polished professional profile. But, you need both.

Let's look first at the networking aspects then we'll explore professional groups, company pages, and job postings. Finally, we'll go through the details about bringing your profile into the All-Star category.

Professional Network

From the granddaddy of them all, Facebook, to Google+, Twitter, Snapchat and many more, social networking is how we communicate and stay in touch with friends, family, and also professional colleagues. Those channels can all be viable means of connecting with people as part of your job search.

But the premier professional network is LinkedIn.

It's where you can connect with those you've met at tradeshows, colleagues in the office, as well as teachers and professors from your college days. The people search function is truly useful in this regard. You can narrow the geographic area, organization, etc. to find those you've worked with over the years and connect.

The job search recommendation is to build your network to at least 500. This is where the connection counter on your profile will top out. It will read 500+. This number will help you show up in recruiter searches. It will also help you find links to people you'd like to contact to learn more about any company that you're trying to penetrate.

People Search
On LinkedIn click the "advanced" search function. The Advance People Search will allow you to use keywords, first and last name, title, company, school, industry, and location to zero in on connections.

This can help you find past and current colleagues and add them to your network. It can also help you find people who are in the company and even the department of a position of interest.

Connection Network
As just one example of using connections in your job search, in Jim's search he was trying to learn more about a small nonprofit. He could find just two people on LinkedIn that had this organization on their profiles. For one of them, he found a direct connection who he had met in a job search focus group.

He reached out to him and he was helpful enough to forward Jim's request to his connection. While Jim didn't make that direct connection, he did get a response from the recruiter! He learned later that all employees were told to forward such requests to the recruiter for follow up. So, a web of connections helped Jim make the critical connection he was seeking.

Education Networking

If you have a college education, it could well be one of the first things that you'd indicate on your LinkedIn account. Once you indicate where you went to college, a link is created between your LinkedIn profile and the university's profile. This creates one of the second biggest networking tools on LinkedIn.

To use this tool search your university in the tool bar. Once you go onto the university's LinkedIn profile you will find that you can search through all of the university's past and present college graduates by their location, place of work, occupation, major, and how you are connected to them.

You are able to click on any of the categories and LinkedIn will refine the search to narrow down the fellow alumni.

Finally once you have selected all you're desired categories, LinkedIn will let you know who your fellow alumni are at your desired company, department, and career. Once you identify these connections you can reach out to them through InMail or through a fellow connection.

This tool can also help you see which companies are looking for someone with your degree / experience or specific university training.

Professional Groups

The next level of connection is through LinkedIn Groups. There are all manner of groups that have been established on LinkedIn. They can be groups that exist outside of LinkedIn, such as professional organizations. They can be groups that exist only on LinkedIn, such as discussion groups around a particular topic.

The job search recommendation is that you join at least 50 groups. You should also select a few and become active in the discussions. All this gets your profile showing up in recruiter searches.

It is also helpful when you want to make a connection outside your range of first level contacts. If you share a group with the person you're trying to contact, that is a perfect way to open the connection. Moreover, LinkedIn allows you to make that invitation to connect directly since you're in the same group.

If you're really ambitious, you can create your own group and invite people to it. It can be about a topic or area of your choice. It's a simple matter to launch the group. It will be more challenging to grow it and maintain it.

Company Pages

There are also company pages on LinkedIn. In fact, any time someone enters a company on their profile it links to that company page. As an example, Jim has created one for PathForeWord.

For your job search the big benefit is that you can follow companies of interest. In addition, they will often post jobs on LinkedIn. Plus, they help you find connections within the company for your further research and contact.

Job Postings

Another huge benefit of LinkedIn is their job postings. You can search these openings based on your key words. You can save those searches and run them on a scheduled basis.

LinkedIn will also alert you to openings that match your search criteria. Furthermore, some job postings actually identify the recruiter that posted the job. So you can reach out to directly promote your candidacy for the position.

Individual Profiles

Given all the power of networking within LinkedIn, none of it works if you don't have a polished professional profile. It's really like having a resume on steroids.

As noted earlier there are now over 400 million users on LinkedIn. So you can imagine that a few best practices have been determined. Let's look first at why you should expend the effort necessary for an All-Star profile and then how to do it.

You Are Who You Appear to Be

"You are who you appear to be." We're quoting the guy that hired Jim to take on massive challenges at a training development operation. At first Jim was stunned. Shouldn't people look beyond appearances to find the "real" person? Isn't there more to who we are than our appearance?

Perhaps. But in the lightning world of recruiting and hiring, people don't have time, or better said, don't take the time to move beyond appearances. You can find the research in the resume section of this book that revealed recruiters spend six-seconds reviewing your resume. We call it "your six-second casting call."

So appearances are important. While you can address that requirement with your superbly crafted cover letter and resume, both targeted at the specific position and organization you're pursuing, it is often your LinkedIn profile that will be used as follow-on information by recruiters. It is also your LinkedIn profile that will be searched by recruiters, and others, looking to fill important positions that you haven't even heard about.

Complete Profile

Users with complete profiles are 40 times more likely to receive opportunities through LinkedIn. Yet only 51% have completed their profiles. Given this, completing your profile to the All Star status gives you a big advantage.

Search results on LinkedIn are ranked based on:

1. Profile completeness
2. Shared connections
3. Connections by degree, first or second, etc.
4. Groups in common

So it makes a great deal of sense to spend some time fully completing your profile, in addition to building your network.

Profile Editing

So let's get down to editing that all important LinkedIn Profile. The first thing to do is select "Edit Profile." At the right hand side of the page where it says "Notify Your Network" select "No."

Otherwise, every change will be broadcast to your network of connections – the 500+ list of contacts that you are growing. When you've completed this round of editing, change the setting to broadcast changes to your connections. Then make one more change to alert them that your profile has been updated.

Profile Settings

This is also a good time to look over your profile privacy settings. You can find this when you mouse over the photo in the upper right hand of the page and selecting "Privacy and Settings."

The only thing we would note here is that you should turn off your activity broadcasts while you're editing your profile, as noted above. Also under "select what others see when you view their profile" opt for "your name and headline." Otherwise you will not be able to see who has viewed your profile.

This is something that you'll want to monitor as you apply for positions. Often times after you've applied for a position you can actually see that the recruiter has viewed your profile. Then you have another connection to pursue – a connection that's actively interested in your background.

Profile Photo

At the top of your LinkedIn profile is your photo. Since this is a professional networking site, your photo should also be professional. Try not to match your Facebook photo. You know the one where you cropped out the other people in the photo just to capture your own head shot – too bad about the arm that is wrapped around your shoulder in that photo.

Take the time to capture a professional photo. You don't have to schedule a sitting with a professional photographer.

One of our local social media experts tells the story of giving his wife his cellphone and having her take literally hundreds of photos of him while moving around the house and posing with different expressions. Out of that, he captured just the right look for his dynamic LinkedIn profile.

My own photo was taken at a business conference where a vendor set up portrait lighting along with a professional photographer and offered free profile photos in exchange for contact information.

One further note on your profile photo – use your keywords in your file name. We were amazed to hear about this search optimization technique at a workshop. It makes sense. You want your name and your keywords everywhere. Your profile photo filename is one more opportunity to turn recruiter searches in your direction.

Background Image

You can also add a background photo to your profile. You'll need an image that's 1400 by 425 pixels. It should be professional and reflect you or your industry. You can find images available through online services or you can make your own, either with online tools or other image software.

At the top of your profile, mouse over the area at the top and select "edit background." Then upload the image of your choice. Make sure you verify that it's working. Your profile is always live. So make sure it's just right.

Public Profile URL

Make sure you've updated your LinkedIn Public Profile URL with a strong username.

When you first set up your account, LinkedIn assigned your profile a number. You can edit that by clicking on "Edit" near the URL information directly under your profile photo. It will tell you if your selection is available when you attempt to edit it.

Once you have a more user-friendly profile URL, you can add it to your resume, business cards, etc.

Contact Information

Next to the URL is the button to edit your contact information. Jim elected to include all his contact information including phone number, email address, and physical address. You can also provide links to your Twitter account and any websites, such as your blog.

Jim also includes this contact information in the profile Summary. You want to take every opportunity to help the recruiter make contact with you about that next career adventure.

Compelling Headline

Well, we've spent a great deal of time on some details. Now we get into the content of your profile. But first a word from our sponsor – branding.

"You are who you appear to be." And so much of who you appear to be is about your personal branding. If you haven't already starting thinking this way while preparing your resume and cover letters, now is a good time to start.

Everything that is posted on this profile is about your personal brand. That branding work must start with your compelling headline. You only have so many words to use in this space.

Jim has chosen to use his personal branding statement "Freelance Writer | Communicator| Blogger." Jim uses this same statement on his resume, website, business cards, etc. It also helps with his one-minute (or is it 30-second?) elevator speech.

Work on that headline until you find one that really fits your personal brand. BTW – this is his fourth or fifth brand statement. The first was Communicator | Organizer | Builder. This fit his early goal of obtaining a director level position. Now he's focused on his freelance and consulting business.

Next in this section is your Location and Industry. Jim selected the broader geographical location – the Dallas/Fort Worth area. This is because recruiters can better relate to this area over his hometown of Grapevine, which could be in any part of Texas for all they know.

If you have considerable experience, selecting an industry can prove challenging as your career may have included many areas. It's best to pick the broadest category that best aligns with your current career goals.

Action-Packed Summary
If the Summary section isn't shown on your profile, add it from the list at the right of your profile. This is a completely open block of text that you can use to really sell your skills and demonstrate how you can solve problems for potential employers.

This is also where you can list your keywords. Finally, you can use it to provide your contact information.

We suggest searching through other LinkedIn profiles in your industry to see examples of how people are sharing their personal message and, yes, their personal branding, in their summary. Then using those examples as inspiration, draft your own that sell your skills and experience to potential employers.

Note that you can also add links or upload files to your Summary, as well as all the other content blocks on LinkedIn. Jim's chosen to provide a link to his visual resume on YouTube and to provide a PDF file of his executive biography.

Experience

The next item on your profile should be Experience. Note that you can move these items around by grabbing the up/down arrow on the far right and dragging that section up or down on your profile.

This applies to all the major categories as well as the individual items, such as positions within your experience.

I suggest leading with your Summary, followed by Experience. However, if you're a recent college graduate, you may want to lead with your Education.

Next add your positions, with dates of employment, company, etc. to your experience.

Here you can take a bit more time providing details about your accomplishments in each position versus what you can do on a resume.

You can also add links and files to each of the positions. On some of Jim's positions he has chosen to add reports or presentations. This is an opportunity to show off your best work. Plus, this is something you can't readily do on a resume or cover letter.

We will note that you can use LinkedIn as a repository for all your experience. This can often help your mindset when you're trying to build a pinpoint resume. The resume can take the key messages forward to generate interest. Your LinkedIn profile can carry all your experience.

This approach often makes Jim's clients feel better about narrowing the focus of the resume. In addition, when you list all your experience and companies on LinkedIn, it opens up further opportunities for networking with past colleagues.

Education

If you've been in the workforce for a considerable amount of time, our big recommendation around Education is to not show the dates unless you have a compelling reason to do so.

For example, even though Jim's education is relatively recent, he earned his degrees well after he started his career, it is still so last century. There is no need to date yourself and have a recruiter consciously or unconsciously rule you out before you've even been considered.

However, if you're on the opposite end of the time scale, or a recent graduate, the dates can be important to show that you have recent training and expertise.

Skills and Endorsements

The Skills and Endorsements section lists those skills where someone else on LinkedIn has endorsed you. It can become quite a long list. Your choices here are whether to display them and where to display them in your profile. You can also elect to add or delete skills. You have an overall limit of showing 50.

Recommendations

LinkedIn also allows written recommendations that can be displayed on your profile. These are directly associated with positions shown on your profile.

Jim has recommendations for nearly every position. We've always thought that this is one of the more powerful features of LinkedIn.

We recommend that you ask some of your key connections to provide written recommendations. They only need to be a few words. Plus, you can either suggest to them a few keywords that they should use in your recommendation or even provide them some language that they can use, modify, or discard.

This is something for you to consider as you're building your profile.

Volunteer Experiences and Causes

Another category of information that you can add to your profile is "Volunteer Experiences and Causes." If you don't have much going on in this space, there is no need to display it on your profile.

Volunteer experience can directly apply to potential positions and assignments. Plus, it shows you give back to your community and industry. That can be important to many employers.

Other Categories

There are a number of other categories of information that you can add to your profile. For example, Groups that you belong to can be sorted and selected to be visible on your profile or not.

Jim's added an extensive listing of Publications to his profile, since that's a big part of what he does as a freelance writer. You may want to list Courses of special note for your professional or personal development. Projects could also be an interesting category to add.

We have used Test Scores to highlight our StrengthsFinders top five strengths. So this gives you an idea of how to use some of these categories to enhance your overall presentation on this important platform.

Resume Builder Tool
We're not big fans of the resume builder tool. But it is an easy way to move your comprehensive LinkedIn profile into a Word document. Once in Word, you can start editing your resume into the laser-focused document you need for each position.

Premium Membership
At roughly $30 per month, premium LinkedIn membership is a serious investment. It offers some helpful tools including direct messaging to recruiters, who's viewed your profile covering the past 90 days along with insight into how they found you, plus you can submit applications as a featured applicant and gain insight into how you compare with other applicants.

It's something you may want to consider to help in your job search.

"You are who you appear to be"
This phrase is so apt when it comes to your LinkedIn profile. Spend some time now and return often to update your profile.

If you're not currently engaged in the job search process, you will be at some point in the future. So take the time right now to start building your profile as well as establishing and refining your personal brand.

Furthermore, don't be afraid to change your personal branding and presentation. You're always gaining new insight and developing your perspective on who you really are and/or want to become. LinkedIn is a great way to get that down in writing and try it out.

Resume Tips

The resume is your starting point for job search. Ideally, it's coming from your LinkedIn profile, but trimmed down quite a bit.

Your Six-Second Casting Call

Once with the recruiter, if you're fortunate enough to get your resume in front of the recruiter, they will be spending roughly six seconds with each resume. Oh my goodness! It doesn't sound like much time does it? All of which means you need to better understand how to reach that recruiter with your message.

Using "gaze trace analysis" here's where the recruiter spends their time with your resume.

Jim Wilson

Communicator | Organizer | Builder

jbwilson@me.com
www.linkedin.com/in/jbwilson

Grapevine, TX (DFW Area)
682-555-5555 mobile

Communications and Publishing Executive

Communicator: written + spoken word | Organizer: teams + projects | Builder: organizations + people.

Action-oriented, hands-on leader of publishing organizations across all types of media. Extensive experience with high-volume operations with hundreds of projects in play all with tight budget and deadline requirements. Experienced with magazine production and financial reporting. Excellent communicator and team builder.

Project Leadership	Publishing Management	Strategic Planning
Organizational Development	Change Management	Product Development
Team Building	Financial Analysis	Statistical Analysis
Brand Management	Volunteer Leadership	Web and Social Media

Experience

BOY SCOUTS OF AMERICA, Irving, TX
National Council with 2.7 million members, 1 million volunteer leaders, $200 million total revenue.

Director Communication Services — 2011-2013
- Responsible for producing all publications, print collateral, websites, videos, multimedia training. Includes Boy Scout Handbook, 130 merit badge pamphlets, www.scouting.org, recruiting campaigns.
- 30 staff members supported by contractors, freelancers, and offshore production.
- Produce 1,200 projects each year for 150 internal clients.
- Operating budget $4 million, purchasing $5 million in printing Roughly 50% of product output generated $16 million in annual gross revenue from literature sales.
- Strategic Organization Transformation ---
  - Added advertising agency skill sets and projects to existing base of technical publishing.
  - Hired first creative director. Ramped up client-focused account management skills.
  - Installed new project management and billing system.
  - Internal Teamwork Effectiveness survey showed 31% gain 2011 to 2012.

Director Media Services & Public Relations — 2008-2011
- Directed 24-person Media Studio operation responsible for all print, web, and video production.
- Responsible for public relations, media relations, internal communications, 100th Anniversary Project, and the National Scouting Museum. Staff size 16 in this area.
- Directed the Executive Visibility Program across extensive Chief Scout Executive travel schedule, developing speeches, and orchestrating events.
- Established first internal communication function and grew it from one to three staff members.
- 100th Anniversary Project included events and activities across the nation. Celebrated two-millionth Eagle Scout, Scout postage stamp and coin, Jamboree, and Adventure Base 100 tour.

21

Director Custom Communication Division and Associate Publisher — 1992-2008
- Directed 60 employees in all print, web, and video production for 100 internal clients.
- Responsible for production of the Boy Scout retail catalog as well as *Boys' Life* and *Scouting Magazine* production and financial reporting.
- Annual budget $7 million plus purchasing $11 million printing, 1,500 projects each year.
- Project Highlight
  - Led team of 40 to revise 119 merit badge pamphlets from one-color to four-color.
  - Revised 9,500 pages, 11,000 images/photos, 1.4 million books printed.
  - Total project cost $1.5 million, completed on time over a 12-month time frame.
- Division Formation Highlights
  - Merged three operations into single internal publishing/communication division.
  - Implemented publishing technology, reduced staff 14%, increased billable time 100%, achieved in excess of $2 million annual savings.
  - Implemented customer satisfaction measures and moved from 69% to 90% in two years, followed by steady improvement to 97% four years later.

Education

MBA in Finance and Marketing
Dallas Baptist University, Dallas, TX

MA in Management
Nazareth College, Kalamazoo, MI

BAS in Electronics Engineering Technology
Siena Heights University, Adrian, MI

We've placed boxes over the three places they felt were the most critical:

- The top of the resume looking at your objective/summary.
- The most recent chronological position.
- Education, typically at the bottom of the final page of the resume.

There are a few other key items, mostly around recent positions, but these are the big ones. They essentially identify the key real estate on your resume.

Pin-Point Focus

You also need to directly match your resume with the job opening.

First, go through the job posting, highlighting all the key items for that position.

Second, the first title of your resume (summary) needs to reflect the title of the position.

Then, all key words and accomplishments need to be focused on the key items for that position.

Your other accomplishments, though of considerable interest to you, are really not of interest to the recruiter. After all, they have only six seconds to place your resume in the stack for further consideration!

This might be tough medicine to swallow for most of us. But, it is right on the mark. The hallmark of any worthwhile communication program is its laser focus on the audience. With your resume, the audience is first the scanning machine and software, then the recruiter, and finally the hiring manager.

All three are looking for key words and matching accomplishments. Of further keen interest is that the first two in this sequence have a list of the key words but don't necessarily know their meaning. Nor would they be able to pick out otherwise applicable experience from your resume. This means you have to hit those same keywords or get tossed. The good news — the key words are in their job description.

Showcase Your Skills

Once you've identified the key skills that the employer is looking for, it is important to put those skills at the top of your resume. Creating a section to showcase your skills is one of the best formatting options. See the box in the resume below.

Brooke Wilson

Brooke.Wilson@me.com
LinkedIn.com/in/brookewilson1

817-555-5555
Amarillo, Texas

Ambitious Student Affairs Professional
Education

Tarleton State University
Master of Science in Management & Leadership
2014 Most Outstanding Student for Department of Management. GPA: 4.0/4.0
- First and only student in the College of Business to research and write a thesis
Bachelor of Science in Psychology, Minor: Management
- Degree completed in 3 years. Honors: Magna Cum Laude

Stephenville, Texas
May, 2014

May, 2012

Qualifications

- Successful experience working on and leading a collaborative team to impact the organization
- Takes initiative in high stress situations with the ability to find effective new solutions quickly
- Demonstrates high level of performance and problem solving with data analysis
- Experienced in academic and business settings with keen insight into data analysis, student relations and organizational behavior

Experience

Career Information Specialist
West Texas A&M University –A member of the Texas A&M System
Canyon, Texas
- Partners in reviewing student resumes and presenting resume workshops
- Collection and analysis of all student first destination graduation data, producing analysis on over 2500 individuals
- Develops info graphics from extensive data into easy to comprehend formats for students and university wide use

September 2015 – Current

Purchasing Administrator
Ryland Homes – Nation's 7th largest homebuilder
- Manage vendor insurance programs and billing
- Administered all purchases for new home starts in 2015
- Maintain and trained in JDE purchasing system
- Accounting research as required

January 2014 – July 2015
San Antonio, Texas

Purchasing Coordinator
Gehan Homes - Top 30 Homebuilder in the Nation
- Managed and oversaw individual purchasing accounts/houses
- Conducted weekly margin reports
- JD Edwards training and experience

June 2013 – October 2013
San Antonio, Texas

Communication Assistant
Henderson Junior High – Stephenville ISD
- Provided American Sign Language Interpretation for a deaf student
- Gained experience in modifying curriculum and teaching

August 2012 – June 2013
Stephenville, Texas

Activities / Honors

- Lions Club Canyon, TX
- Sigma Phi Lambda Alumni Council
- "Internet Dependency and Academic Performance"
  Published in *Journal of Social Media in Society* V4, No. 1

Member 2015 - present
Summer 2014 – present

2015

This section can be referred to as a skills or qualifications section. It's important to show the employer within the first six seconds that you possess the exact skills they are seeking.

Think of your resume as a billboard. When driving down the highway at 75 mph the billboards that catch your eyes are simple and to the point. Restaurants advertise the one or two products they know the consumers want. If a restaurant placed their entire menu on the billboard, there is little chance anyone would take the time to read it. The same goes for your resume.

The desired key words have been identified; your personal qualifications have been pinpointed and now its time to create powerful statements that will win over the employer. It is key to start each statement in this section with an action verb or a number. By starting with an action verb, power and importance are instilled within the statements. This will show the employer that you are action oriented and you get the job done in the areas that are of most concern to them.

Quantifying your qualifications showcases knowledge and dedication in the areas that are currently an empty void within the employer's office. These two things will help set your resume apart from the pack.

Cover Letters

Jim's first big take away from career workshops, particularly those run by recruiters themselves, was that cover letters are not typically even read. They may be glanced at before going on to the resume.

However, they did note that if the cover letter is formatted in what's known as a T format, then they will get more than a glance and may be skimmed by the recruiter.

The T format cover letter is formatted into two columns. The first column covers the stated requirements of the job. The second column covers how your experience addresses each of those requirements.

Since learning this little bit of information, we've always provided a T format cover letter. We will also note that the work you spend on this type of cover letter is a great way to get started in customizing your resume for each job application.

Brooke Wilson

Brooke.Wilson@me.com
LinkedIn.com/in/brookewilson1

Mobile 817-555-555
San Antonio, Texas

Date: 16 June 2015

Subject: Career Information Specialist

I am seeking to relocate to the Amarillo area and spotted your opening for a Career Information Specialist. I feel my experience and education are an excellent fit while my motivation and approach to work would make me an excellent employee.

While earning my undergraduate and graduate degrees from a Texas A&M university at Tarleton State I found a passion for small town schools and the A&M System. I feel that this position would be an excellent opportunity to gain experience at the university level while applying my research, analysis, data reporting, communication, and organizational skills to the tasks of the position.

Here's a brief summary of my background:

Approach to Work	I completed my undergraduate degree in three years. I'm also the first thesis candidate in the college of business for Tarleton State University. This was based on my passion for research, analysis, and communicating the results. I also feel I can contribute within an academic environment as well as relate to faculty, staff, and students.
Work Experience:	I'm currently working for a large homebuilder where I gather, analyze, and produce reports on a daily basis. I am familiar with JD Edwards and SPSS Analysis. I have managed large amounts of research data during my thesis and undergraduate data collection. I also work well in a team environment – working hard and having fun.
Assisting Students:	I currently advise a sorority at Tarleton State University where I help develop college age students for their lives during and after college. Reviewing written material is also a strong skill, which would benefit student resume development.
Presentation/Organization:	Conferences and presentations are one of my passions. I have spoken at many conferences and am a strong public speaker. I maintain a very organized schedule and find joy in planning and facilitating workshops and events. In those situations, I handle the pressure and come up with on-demand solutions to the inevitable problems you can encounter.

While I feel strongly that the written word can communicate a great deal, I also feel that face-to-face communication is the best way to gain insight into people and their backgrounds. With that in mind, let's get on the phone, or meet in person, to discuss my background, my skills, my approach to work and how I can bring them to how I can bring them to West Texas A & M University.

Sincerely

Brooke Wilson

Add Your Cover Letter to Your Resume

Another way that you can use cover letters is to include them as the first page of your resume in the file you submitted online.

We like this approach a great deal. After all, you've spent a great deal of time on both the cover letter and the resume. You want to make sure that the recruiter and the hiring manager see all the pertinent information.

Give that option consideration the next time you forward your cover letter and resume.

Email Options — Your Virtual Handshake
Another approach is to consider the cover letter as a virtual handshake by transferring the content of your cover letter into a format that has a better chance of being noticed and read by a recruiter — copy and paste it into an email, with your resume attached.

Follow Up – Follow Up
Once you've applied for a position online or through networking made a connection, it is critical to follow up. Constructing the T formatted cover letter as mentioned above and then copying the content and pasting it within an email and sending it to the employer or network contact will ensure you make a good connection and help you transition into a future conversation with the employer.

Brooke's experience is a superb case in point. She built her resume and cover letter, forwarded it online through the formal application process, but she didn't stop there. She found the hiring manager and forwarded the virtual handshake email, built from her cover letter, along with her resume.

The hiring manager responded to schedule an interview. She also asked that Brooke apply online. When Brooke informed her that she already applied online, the hiring manager was astounded to find that Brooke's application never made it to her.

Lesson – find several ways to get in front of the hiring manager. Then schedule some follow up contact points and methods.

Interview Tips

Ideally your resume and cover letter have done their main job, securing an interview. That most likely will be a phone interview or maybe even a Skype interview. And, if that goes well, you can expect an in person interview.

So, what are you going to say during your interview? You'll need to focus on what you can do for your prospective employer. While you may think the interview is all about you, it's actually about how you can help your future employer.

The best way of demonstrating what you can do is to talk about what you've done in the past to bring success to your employer's projects. Given that, your interview become all about how you tell stories.

S-T-A-R Stories
The S-T-A-R approach is all about building stories around:

- Situations you've encountered in your career.
- Tasks that you've addressed.
- Actions that you've taken.
- Results that you've achieved, ideally with measurements.

I have usually combined the Tasks and the Actions into a single step.

The point is to look at the key competencies, skills, and experiences you need to excel in the open position. Then prepare S-T-A-R stories that demonstrate those things in action — proving not only that you can do the job but that you have already done elements of the job and done so successfully.

Having a short scripted response for each of the S-T-A-R items can also help you feel confident in your message and ensure that you address the critical items of each story.

Plus, it will get you into telling engaging stories all about what you accomplished and what you can do for your next employer. Those stories will be remembered and bring you to the top of the employer's mind when comparing candidates.

Note, too, that you will probably encounter two general types of interviews. Some interviewers will ask for specific examples that tie into the current job opening. Those will be easy to address with your S-T-A-R stories.

Others interviewers will only ask general questions. In that case, address that question and then transition into the most suitable S-T-A-R story to demonstrate how you've handled those situations in the past and will in the future.

The important thing is to get the message across — I can do this job, here's why.

Questions to Expect

These questions were developed for Jim's interviewing process, generally for candidates that had been previously qualified through skill testing and rigorous interviews by the direct hiring manager.

Jim's role was to provide a second or third interview that allowed the direct hiring manager to sit to one side and just watch. Typically, there would be two finalists and this was a great way to get the direct hiring manager off the spot, allowing them to really see the candidates in direct comparison.

With that framework in mind, Jim developed these questions not to pose technical issues or address job skills, but instead to see how well each candidate could think and communicate. Here are the key questions that he used during those sessions.

1. Tell me about yourself. Why did you choose this type of work?
2. What attracts you to this position? How does this position relate to your past work/career experience?
3. What things in your job do you feel that you have done particularly well, or in which you have achieved the greatest success? For what things have your managers complimented you?
4. What is the area in which you would most like to improve? What aspects of your previous jobs gave you the most trouble?
5. What was your biggest failure in your last job?
6. Wherever you worked before, what made it a good day?
7. What are some of the things you would like to avoid in a job and why?
8. How do you define teamwork? Give an example of a project that you have worked on that shows experience in working in a team environment.
9. What kind of people do you find most difficult to work with? How have you been successful in those situations?
10. Describe how you determine your priorities on your current job. Give me a specific example of how you schedule your time on an unusually hectic day.

11. Give me an example of a time when you had to go above and beyond the call of duty in order to get a job done.
12. What kind of person is your supervisor? What are your supervisor's greatest strengths? In what areas could they have done a better job?
13. If I were your supervisor, what would be the most important thing for me to say or do to support you?
14. If you were hiring someone for this job, what qualities would you look for?
15. Let's assume for a minute that you have one concern about accepting this job. What is that one concern?
16. What is one question that we didn't ask you today during your interview? And what would your answer be?
17. Why should we hire you?

Use these questions for practice when you're getting ready for your interview. Combined with your S-T-A-R stories, you should be very well prepared.

Questions to Ask

Often overlooked as you prepare for an interview is what questions you should ask of the interviewer. This is your golden opportunity to first surface any issues that the interviewer may have that you need to get out in the open and address. Second, you can learn more about the position, the organization, and the interviewer. And, third, it is your opportunity to impress the interviewer with your thoughtful questions.

After all, your interviewer has already heard their questions and most of the answers before. It's your questions that will bring something new to the conversation.

On the first point above, we always like to ask if the interviewer has any concerns at this stage of the process. This quite often surfaces some hidden concerns that are quietly resting below the surface and getting ready to send your prospects to the bottom of the ocean.

Getting them out in the open allows the interviewer to candidly express them and allows you to address them. Don't ever pass up the opportunity to ask this most critical of questions. Of course, if the concern is truly a deal breaker that you can't overcome, it does help you prepare for your next interview...

As always your key focus should be on the organization's needs. Then you can focus on how you can use your expertise, experience, and enthusiasm to meet those needs. Here's an opening list of questions that we've prepared as we get ready for an interview:

1. How did the opening occur?
2. What were the previous person's best attributes in the position? Any improvements you'd like to see?
3. What are the key goals for this position, for the organization?
4. What do you want accomplished in the first 60, 90, and 120 days?
5. What are the biggest stumbling blocks to expect?
6. Are there any gaps between what we've discussed and what you're seeking? Any concerns at this point?
7. What are the next steps in the search process?

That next to last question zeros in on one way of articulating the question — are there any concerns with me that I can address? This, then, allows you to surface these concerns and then work toward addressing them at once as well as when you get further into the selection process.

Job Search Campaign

So far we've been talking about all the tools you need in your job search. So of those tools, like networking and LinkedIn, you'll be using throughout your career. Others you'll be developing for specific campaigns and, at a more granular level, for each specific position. This includes resume, cover letter, and developing interview stories.

Yes, this is a campaign. It needs your attention as well as a detailed plan of attack.

Set Goals

At the beginning of every journey it's important to know where you're going. If you don't know that, you'll find yourself wandering all over looking for that next opportunity and quite possibly wasting your time.

Of course, there are opportunities that will appear that you weren't expecting. Yet, somehow they will be connected first with your network and more typically with the messages that you've been sending to your network about your search.

So, ideally you're setting some goals around location, industry, organization, and position plus timeframe. This then starts to narrow your focus and help you better leverage your time and your resources.

Build a Plan

Once you've set your goals, you can develop a plan of attack that is designed to meet those goals. Your plan doesn't have to be elaborate or all that detailed. But it is important to get something down in writing.

Even as it changes based on new information or other opportunities, you'll at least have something to update. This can then serve as not only a plan but also as an important benchmark to consult throughout your search.

Track Your Activity

We recommend building a document that records your search activities. This can be a simple as a spreadsheet with entries on what you've done, the results, and what comes next.

During Jim's early outplacement search, he recorded nearly 300 items over the first six months. Many of these were records of contacts made, coffee meetings, workshops, applications submitted, etc.

All this not only helped jog his memory from time to time but also served as a useful reminder of follow up actions. It also served as a record of what was accomplished during the search.

Sometimes it can seem like you're making little to no progress. It's well to go back to the list of actions and as a result bolster your spirits that you are taking the right steps and a breakthrough has to happen soon.

Preparation and Practice

Finally, a big part of your job search campaign needs to be about preparation and practice. With preparation, it's all about developing your resume and cover letters for each specific position. Then it's about preparing your interview stories and practicing them in front of someone else or, lacking that, in front of a mirror.

For those of you who are early in your careers, preparing and practicing your interview stories will be pretty straightforward. You'll no doubt have ready recall of the key aspects and the impact measures of your work. Even so, you'll need to practice to ensure that your story telling is flawless.

For those of you with lengthy careers, it may well take some digging to bring up your stories for various stages of your career that best fit the position you've targeted for the next stage. That takes digging through your records, bringing up old memories, and assembling that perfect story that conveys your skills, your approach, and the impact you can bring to the new position.

In either of those scenarios, it's practice that polishes your performance during the interview. It also serves to overcome any lingering nervousness. If you're prepared, you can knock this out of the park.

Summary

As you look back over this book, you can tell that we feel that LinkedIn is a vital part of not only your job search, but also you're entire career. It is key to networking and a big part of that is reaching out in your industry and your profession to improve your job search prospects and to help others in their job search.

Resumes, cover letters, and to a certain extent even interviews are but tools in your job search. It's the networking that will continue to help you in your current job search, your career, and in future job search efforts.

Plus, at one point in your career, if not already, you'll be doing the hiring. Networking will be critical in finding just the right people for your team.

We wish you the best in your job search and trust that this small book will be helpful along the way.

Brooke and Jim